Onedia N. Gage

In Purple Ink
Poetry for the Spirit

In Purple Ink

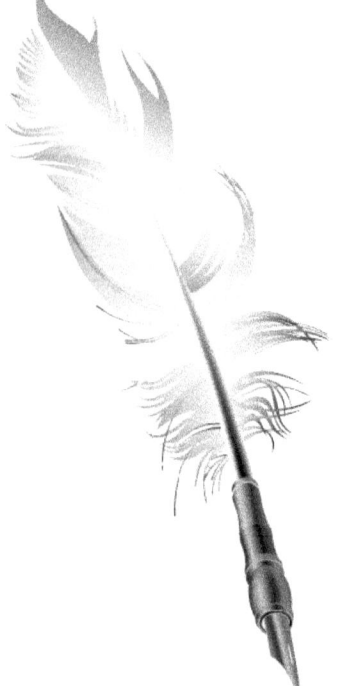

In Purple Ink
Poetry for the Spirit

Onedia N. Gage

Purple Ink, Inc Press
Houston, TX

In Purple Ink
Poetry for the Spirit

All Rights Reserved © 2010 Onedia N. Gage

No part of this of book may be reproduced or transmitted in
Any form or by any means, graphic, electronic, or mechanical,
Including photocopying, recording, taping, or by any
Information storage or retrieval system, without the
Permission in writing from the publisher.

Purple Ink, Inc. Press

For More Information:
Purple Ink, Inc
P O Box 27242
Houston, TX 77227
www.purpleink.net

ISBN: 978-0-9801002-5-9

Printed in United States

[14]For this reason I kneel before the Father, [15]from whom his whole family in heaven and on earth derives its name. [16]I pray that out of his glorious riches he may strengthen you with power through his Spirit in your inner being, [17]so that Christ may dwell in your hearts through faith. And I pray that you, rooted and established in love, [18]may have power, together with all the saints, to grasp how wide and long and high and deep is the love of Christ, [19]and to know this love that surpasses knowledge—that you may be filled to the measure of all the fullness of God. [20]Now to him is able to do immeasurably more than all we ask or imagine, according to his power that is at work within us, [21]to him be glory in the church and in Christ Jesus throughout the generations, forever and ever! Amen.

Ephesians 3:14-21 NIV

[20]Now to Him is able to do immeasurably more than all we ask or imagine,
Ephesians 3:20a

His power that is at work within you through Christ Jesus!
Ephesians 3:20b

In Purple Ink

DEDICATION

To Hillary Nicole
And ALL Daughters

May these words address your
Deepest and Most Spiritual
Needs

In Purple Ink

TABLE OF CONTENTS

A Kinship With God	14
On My Knees	15
When I Kneel Before You	16
In His Presence	17
The Hem of His Garment	18
Five Minutes to Empty	19
A Hero Departs	20
Yielded Unto You	21
The Full Circle of Life	22
When I Die	23
Your Testimony	24
Pieces of a Dream	26
Thou Shall Love	27
In Bigger Hands	28
As Is	29
The Holiday Season	30
Letter to an Atheist	31
What Is Your Thumb?	32
Nehemiah's Gift of Love	33
Nehemiah's Nap	34
Through Children's Eyes	35
Overnight	36
I Appreciate Your Struggles: A Mother's Love	37
To My Mother and Other Mother's Who Read This	39
The Women in My Life	41
Identity Crisis	42
The Private Reconciliation of a Woman	43
Tell Me Your Story	44
Generational Mercies: A Real Life Experience	45
Love	47
The Perfect Husband	48
We Are A Love Story	50
My Knight and Shining Armor	51
One Afternoon	52
Holding My Hand	53
The Layers of His Music	55
For All Dads: Tell Her the Truth	57
The Measure of a Man	59
The Man You Are	61
His Glory	62
The Message	64
Think Think Think	65
Wearing Pink	66

You Hate America	67
(So This Is) Africa	69
Would We Have Come	70
In Purple Ink	71
The Glass House In Which We Live	72
Is Love the Blade of Grass or the Drip of Water	74
A Warrior Mentality	76
Perceived Limits	77
The Nerve To Dream	79
Daydreamer	81
In Search Of	82
Examine Your Life	83
Shedding the Stuff	84
Life Happens	86
Mirror, Mirror	87
The Miracle Before You	88
The Salt from Your Tears is Hypertensive	89
Ninety or Something Close	90
Borrowed Time	91
Clear The Mechanism	92
Legend of Bagger Vance	94
Declaration of Independence	95
Forgiven	96
In Twenty Minutes	97
Attitude In Stanzas	98
Lady In Waiting	99
Puzzles	100
Heart Check	101
In My Shoes	102
Visit Life's Edge	104
The Scent of Your Feet	105
The Heartbeat and Its Version of the Story	106
Separating Memories from Reality	107
Transfer on Death	108
The Family Secrets	109
The One Question I Have	110
Acknowledgements	114
About the Author	116

Onedia N. Gage

In Purple Ink

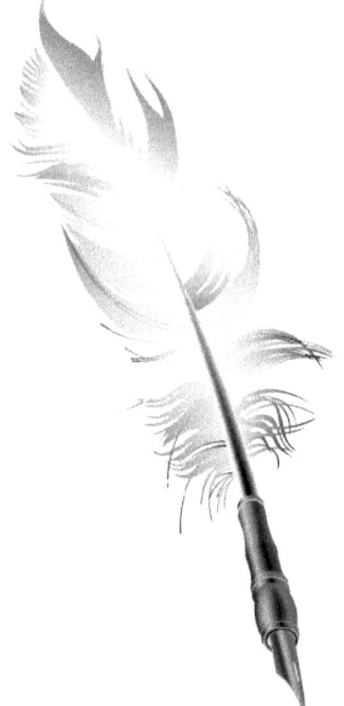

A Kinship with God

Created me from dust
Formed me in her womb
Knew me
Know me
Plans for me

Disciple me
Discipline me
Gifted me
Equipped to serve You

Our love
Our friendship
My disobedience
Your forgiveness

A special communication
. . . prayer
A special encounter
. . . mediation
A special assignment
. . . gifts
A special relationship
. . . a friendship

A relationship where He speaks to me
Where my spirit communes with His
When You consider me
How You hear me

This relationship
       This kinship nurtures my soul
       This kinship captures my spirit
       This kinship ministers to my hurts

The kinship is my life's love
The kinship of God—my refuge.

ON MY KNEES

When I got off of my knees
      . . . I got away from God

Not a good idea
A stupid one indeed
The worst one I have ever had, in fact

Tragedy
Circumstances
Issues
Tissues
      . . . all designed to drive me to my knees
Gifted to me for a super highway back to God.

Storms
Unforgiveness
Sin
Problems
      . . . perfectly planned to reunite me with my Christ

When I got off of my knees
      . . . I got away from God.

Storms are survivable on my knees
Issues are resolved on my knees

On my knees I reach out to God
On my knees I reach God
On my knees I seek God
On my knees I meet God
On my knees I find wise Counsel
On my knees He rescues me from myself

When I am on my knees
      . . . I am closest to God.

When I got off my knees
      . . . I got away from God

A great place
      . . . On My Knees.

When I Kneel Before You

My kneeling equals reverence
        And respect
My kneeling communicates my love
        And loyalty
My kneeling convicts my soul
        And spirit
My kneeling confesses my sins
        And suffering
My kneeling closes the gap between God (Him)
        And me (His results)
My kneeling changes the circumstances
        And convictions
My kneeling keeps me honest
        And humble
My kneeling reminds me of the proximity of the One who sent Him
        And the One who came
My kneeling aligns me to the purpose
        And the passion of God
My kneeling prepare me to work
        And walk on God's walk
My kneeling reconciles me to His Spirit
        And Holy Spirit
When I kneel before You,
        I know You love me!

IN HIS PRESENCE

Humbled
Meek
Bowed
Humility
        Before You

Broken
Sinner
Selfish
Bitter
        In Front of You

Teacher
Preacher
Disciple
Prophet
        With You

Pure
Purposed
Driven
Poised
Polished
        Within Your Presence

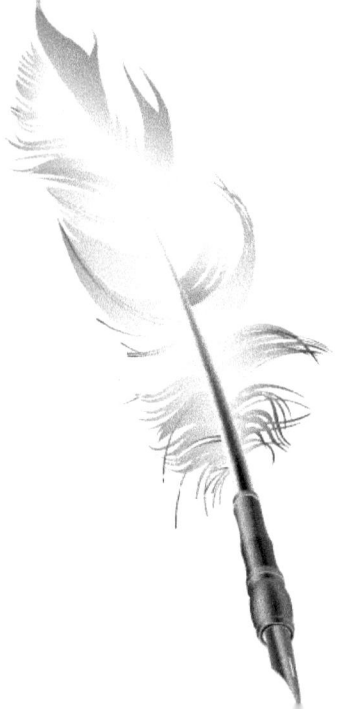

The Hem of His Garment

Make Me Whole
MAKE me whole
Make ME whole
Make me WHOLE

I heard that You could
What must I do to be whole
Where is my access
My access to wholeness

Prayer
Fellowship
Fasting
Repentance
Covenant
Commitment

How long until I am whole?
Whose definition of whole are we using?
This time: lifetime

Need saving now
Emergency plan: ultimate sacrifice
Seek power source

Access starts in His presence
Can you get there—to His presence
When you have time to get there
You gain immediate access to the
Hem of His Garment

Proximity brings forth power

He will make you whole.

FIVE MINUTES TO EMPTY

When the gas light comes on
How many miles do you still drive
Knowing the tank is continuing to empty

How can I feel empty when You fill me?

How can I say that I am empty when
You have never left my soul?

How can I speak as if my heart has
Room for other stuff when You
Have consumed my whole heart?

A HERO DEPARTS

Gone—a now elevated concept
Forever, never felt so sudden, so real
Man
        —Godly
        —strong
        —spirited
        —loving
        —God-fearing
Oh man, my hero
My example, my leader
My life
Touching lives as you trod
Oh hero
You now sit with Him
I will miss
Because of your wisdom, I thank
For your faith, now I believe the unbelievable
For your salvation, I receive abundant blessings
For your kindness, I give abounding love
For your special joy, I embrace
For your mission, I live
For your grace, I love
Because of our long walks, I hear with my heart
Because of your leadership, I am wise and still young.
Because of your prayers, I experience peace.
For your love—abundant and true, I will never forget.
You are my hero
My one and only love.

For Pressy and Corey Bailey

YIELDED UNTO YOU!

I listen
I listen
I try to speak
You speak
You speak firmly
You speak strongly
Sometimes I miss
Sometimes I misunderstand
Sometimes I understand

I obey
I disobey
I know You are talking to me
I deny sometimes
I can hear You
When You speak,
I check for Your voice
I do the work You require
My obedience stirs others
Your spirit stirs within me
Your spirit uses me
Your spirit directs me
Your spirit yields me

I submit to You
I yield to You
I am living a life yielded unto You
I love You
You love me more
Your love causes me to yield to You

Yielded unto You!

THE FULL CIRCLE OF LIFE

When life meets you full circle,
    Where will you be?

Will you be known for kindness and care?
    Or joy and wonder?

Will you be known for change in the lives of others?
    Or the challenge of the status quo?

Could it be you solved one of the world's crisis?
    Or you served the world's underprivileged well?

Will you have traveled the world with His message?
    Or just your community for Him until pale?

Will your labor have advanced His word?
    Or secured His glory?

Will you be known for resistance to wrong?
    Or will you seek justice to stand?

Will your goals all be achieved?
    Or will you just achieve what matters most?

Will you have sacrificed for others when you could've served self?
    Or will the effects of your work be blessed beyond your borders and boundaries?

Keep your head about you and keep your heart ready to give
So that when the life He blessed you with travels full circle,
You will be next to meet with His peace
You will be met with preparedness to meet Him
You will be equipped to praise Him face to face.

Where will you be when your life meets you full circle?

WHEN I DIE

Will the words read "hall of fame"
      Or mystery and shame?
Will the degrees be worth the toil
      Or would sacrifice be foiled?
When I die
      Who will come
           Will they cry
                Because of love
                    Or hurt or hate
Will my ministry live beyond my days
Will my legacy garner Your praise
Will I have made value of my days
When I inspect my life for its worth
I know You destined me for greatness
      Since birth
I don't want to disappoint You
When we face—
      When I am delivered to Your hands.

YOUR TESTIMONY

⁴On the contrary, we speak as men approved by God to the entrusted with the gospel. We are not trying to please men but God, who tests our hearts.

1 Thessalonians 2:4

¹⁰But he knows the way that I take; when he has tested me, I will come forth as gold.

Job 23:10

¹There is a mine for silver and a place where gold is refined.

Job 28:1

What you thought was for your harm
Was used for your good

When the future looked bleak
An foreseen circumstances turned bleak to blessing

When you thought He had turned His back on you
He only turned away to complete plans for you

How can I recover from this disaster you ask
He answered rest in My Sovereignty

What will I do about this scenario
He asked Am I enough to solve your issues?

Your trials
Your tribulations
Your wallowing
Your pain

You are re-writing the definition of limits daily
Where are your boundaries?

That test you took is just a test
This is only a test
Which you will transition into your testimony
A testimony exuding faith,
Eliminating doubt
Eradicating fear
Establishing relationship

Your tests compose your testimony
Your tests create your testimony

Your testimony is the story you tell
Your tests may never be recounted
Your tests may never be repeated

Your testimony is critical
Your tests refine you

Your tests cultivate your testimony.

PIECES OF A DREAM

One piece
Two piece
Four

With glue and paste
A pieced together dream
These pieces sometimes do not fit
I wonder why the picture is not clear not complete
Work in progress, I guess
Pieces of things I like create this dream
The whole picture cannot be seen
That's Daddy's job
But I like the pieces He lets me see
Of the dreams I have
The plans He has for me

Sometimes they seem incongruent and jumbled
Unorganized at best
But just remember
He created the dreams in me
So He can handle the rest.

THOU SHALL LOVE

When He announced His sovereignty
And commanded you to love,
You were to respond with excitement

When He declared His plans for you
And confirmed that you were intentional
Not the mistake you heard you were
You were supposed to rise to the occasion

When He shared His son
To save your life
You were to intertwine yourself with Him

When He gifted you with the Holy Spirit
Who intercedes on your behalf
You were supposed to love Him with your obedience

When He lavished you with forgiveness
Which your undeserving self
You were supposed to love Him with your forgiveness of others

When He offered you His peace
Which transcends your complete understanding
You were supposed to share that peace with others

When He loves you
Which you sometimes reject Him with your disobedience
You were supposed to share that love with others

IN BIGGER HANDS

That does not belong to you
That does not belong to you either

That is not on your job description
That does not fit your skill set

That is not on your resume
That is not your area of expertise

All of it is in Bigger Hands
His hands can handle it

All of it belongs to Him
His hands are designed to handle all of that

All of it is under His control
His hands consider it done

Why are you spending your time on what doesn't belong to you
That belongs to Bigger Hands

As Is

God made me
> But my greatest critic
> Wants me to change

God forgives me
> Yet my warmest love
> Leaves my feelings to the
> Care of another

God hears my cry
> However my one
> Neglects my tears

God promises comfort
> While my significant other
> Provides conditional shelter for my soul

God enhances my sorry self
> When my spouse
> Subjects me to pain

God accepts me As Is
> The way He made me

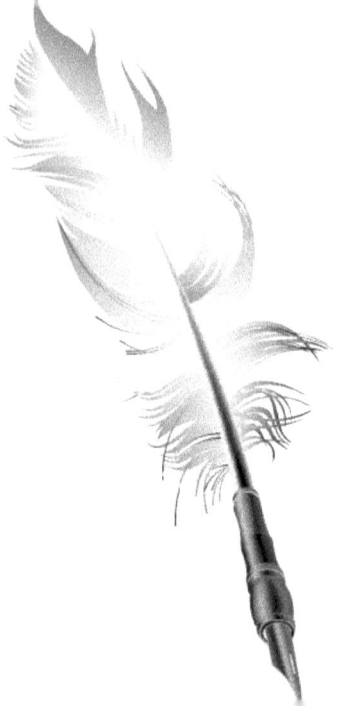

THE HOLIDAY SEASON

During this holiday season
Reflect realizing it was
Birthed of true love.
The spirit of giving
The season of joy
The promise of peace
The provision of hope
The Birth of the Son,
       His Son
This love and this season exist
Despite uncertainty of a Next
Only because of
His love
. . . an unconditional love
Yet matched not even by one.

LETTER TO AN ATHEIST

You ask why we can't keep company.
We simply don't share the common ground we need to share
To be successful as we relate.

Yes, you are right. There are some Christians who
Think the same as you.
They want me in bed too.
Probably worse than you.
The difference is he recognizes
That he is a sinner.
But do you?
You don't consider your wrongdoings as sin.
But Christians while doing wrong will
Someday be convicted for those wrongs and
Will be able to repent.
I pray for your salvation.
I pray for you to receive the Lord as your Savior and lifeline.
I pray you recognize the Lord for who He actually is:
Your Creator.
The One who even allows you the freedom
Of thought to become an
Atheist.

What Is Your Thumb?

Her thumb comforts
She escapes her pain
She examines her issues

Her thumb soothes
She redirects her thoughts
She considers her options

Her thumb secures
She sits behind the security of the thumb
She feels safe with the thumb

Her thumb provides
She seeks solutions with the thumb
She spends time with the thumb

What is your thumb?
What strengthens you?
What subsides your grief?
What soothes you?
What pacifies you?

What is your thumb?

She manages that thumb closely.

She cares for it carefully.

She protects it methodically.

NEHEMIAH'S GIFT OF LOVE

God gives us gifts
Because He loves us
Not by our deserve
Because He planned
Not by our own design

God's gifts are sovereign
Because He is sovereign
Not because we are perfect
Because we are not perfect
Not by any mistake

Nehemiah, we accept you
As a perfect gift from a
Perfect and omniscient God

So gentle
So loving, already

So wonderful
So handsome

So undeserved
So thankful

Nehemiah, the gift you are
Is the love we give

He sent your name
He sent us you
A son, the son
For whom we prayed

So from our love to yours
Thank you for loving us back.

Nehemiah's Nap

The soft sound of rumpled sheets
Eased me out of my dreams
To see you as I rise
Sealed my security
Eliminated my fears
Healed my scars

The whispered I love you
Motivated my heart
Invaded my soul

The sunshine greeted me
Assuring me that
Love awaits me
The fullness of the embrace
The mystery of the future
But the promise of real love

Then you crawled into my space
Settled in
Exhaled
Soft snores followed
I watched love in slow motion
Your security renamed
Your time
Your space
Your comfort

Rest my love rest
Watching you sleep made my heart flutter

Through Children's Eyes

The purity that exists
Which dwells within
Through children's eyes
Tell the story of their life

The innocence that exists
Which expresses their honesty
From children's eyes
Shares their knowledge

The trust that exists
Which develops from their soul
From children's eyes
Communicates the level of trust which inhabits them

The love they need
Which grows within
Through children's eyes
Requests the love they need from you

The love they have
Which they give away freely
Through children's eyes
Shares the love they have for you

The innocence of their eyes
Solves problems
Calms fears
Steals hearts
Stills the soul
Changes minds
Settles disputes

The power they have
Through their eyes
Shapes lives

OVERNIGHT

Overnight you grew
Sometimes in daytime
You grew while I was at work
You changed while I was at the grocery store
When I turned around to pour your milk
You grew
Inch by inch
Pound by pound
You grew
Without notice
Without my consent
You smile bigger
You laugh longer
And louder
Your thoughts deepen
Your knowledge expands
In my presence
Before my very eyes
Tugging on my heart
You grew
Taller
Stronger
Smarter
Happier
I love you

I APPRECIATE YOUR STRUGGLES
A MOTHER'S LOVE

Two jobs
Or Three
Just so that ends can wave at each other
Though they may never meet

Rare love life
So that I'm safe, secured
And spoiled

Restless night
Filled with worry,
Anxiety, fear

Your strengths resemble
None other
But similar to so
Many others

Your health
Left to chance
But mine carefully
Orchestrated

You have walked miles for me
About which I'll never know
You have shed many tears
Of which I may never understand

You have struggled for me
Countless times
On many occasions
For many reasons

Even in my ridiculous-ness
You have defended me
You have loved me
You have been consumed with me
And the concept of me

You have sacrificed much for me
You have struggled because of me
"I would live under the bridge
If it weren't for you."

I appreciate your struggle
I appreciate your sacrifice
I appreciate your dreams for me
I appreciate you!
And who you are to me!

To My Mother And Other Mothers Who Read This

This started out as a poem but grew
Into much more

I stood preparing for my day
Your image remained steady
In my mind
I watch your moves, moods, motions
I wonder what's on your mind
What's in your heart

I think that you are the best
I know that you give your best
And although sometimes
Discouraged, you keep in the race
You set the pace

Although hard, you know that I
Hold a mirror up to you daily
I am your child
Mouth, mannerisms, emotions
In earlier days, you would look
Upon me with disgust
Later I could learn that the
Mirror was there
Don't worry—I've changed some
Of the attributes of the image
But don't forget I love the mirror

Eight years passed since we shared an abode
In my attempt to recapture
Missed moments
Binding and bonding moments

I know that I'm not all that
I need to be
Or that you expected me to be
I know that I have snatched some of your moments
But I'm striving to give them back

Mother, I love you.

Mother, I pray for you

I pray for your health
I pray for your strength
I pray for your heart
I pray for your success
I pray for your wisdom
I pray for your grace
I pray for your spirit
I pray for your struggle

THE WOMEN IN MY LIFE

Bold
Beautiful
Brilliant
Oh yes, she is

She is amazing
Awesome
Authentic

When I walked into her life
She received me with wisdom
Love
Patience

The women in my life
Strong
Stern
Steering

Her distinguished leadership
Her excellent education
Her profound service
Her rich experience

The woman in my life
Loves   encourages
Leads   empowers
Listens   empathizes

The women impart knowledge

I love those women
They hold me up

IDENTITY CRISIS

Her words hit me like cold water
Are you mixed
Are you black
I'm black too
Her identity attached to the shallowest of measures
Yet important, extremely

Searching for an identity match
Same shade
Same smile
Same circumstances
Same passion
Searching for the DNA match

Ordinary enough   to fit in
Unique enough   to raise an eyebrow
Distinct enough   to be set apart

No mother near
Mother figure distant in generations
Distant still in relationship

Consistently searching for answers
Countless searches for feedback
Command attention by any means necessary

Just a little time
Answers to questions
From a wondering mind
From a lonely heart

Just some attention
From the right person
Would propel her forward

Don't shed another tear
You will succeed
Just a little help you need

Quit checking for the identity
In ordinary things
Rather start inside

The identity is in her eyes.

The Private Reconciliation of a Woman

From caterpillar to butterfly
And you were present
And didn't know
And didn't notice
You fell for "fine" and "ok"
When she really meant "broken"
If she thought you could handle the truth
She would've answered "pained"

She transformed before your very eyes
From sweet and gentle to
Bitter and regretful
From independent and decisive to
Insecure and misunderstood
From happy and spirited to
Broken and pained

She is transforming before your very eyes
From bitter and hurt to
Powerful and overjoyed
From lonely and immobile to
Energetic and thoughtful
From disheartened and disadvantaged to
Lighthearted and refreshing

She finally reconciled the past with
Reality
She found balance
Infused strength
Reclaimed herself
Reintroduced herself to the world
As a healing vessel
Empowered herself
Transformed her thoughts
Changed her actions
Corrected her conduct
All privately
Without your attention to a single detail
All in your presence
While you stand amazed
At her private reconciliation

TELL ME YOUR STORY

Tell me
Tell me of your pain
Tell me of your hurt
Tell me of your victory
Your struggles
Your worries
Your dismay

Tell me
I wanna know
I care
I'm concerned

Tell me the details
Of your cancer
Of your remission
Of your miscarriage
Of your miscarriages
Of your adoption
Of your healing
Of your abortions

I can't judge
I can't

I won't judge
I won't

Tell me your story
Tell me your story—I'm listening
Tell me your story—I need to know
Tell me your story—I'm thirsty for your testimony
Tell me your story

Generational Mercies
A Real Life Experience

When I consider the possibilities of my life
The abundance thereof
I could scare
But why wimp out now
Education standard
I want more
I need more

Allergic to mediocrity
My life redefines excellence
My life intimidates others
I could care
But those cares are the opposite of excellence

With both generations watching my every move
My decisions important
Excellence priority
Exercise faith
Explore the impossible
Ignore the naysayers
Avoid the ignorant

Start a new trend
Raise the bar for an excellent generation
Set a new standard
View the high bar as achievable
The sky is the real limit
Not your mind
Not even your heart
Certainly not your physical ability

Escape the mundane
Ostracize the ordinary
Reinvent the talented tenth
From within
Disturb the force
Change the course of those to come
NOW!

I CAN!
LIVE A LIFE OF EXCELLENCE!
I can achieve more and do better
Than the heritage I have

My excellent legacy
Creating a safe place for
Your best work

That's a generational mercy.

LOVE

A different kind of love

The kind of love that picks the lock of your soul

The kind of love that gives you courage

The kind of love that introduces you to wholeness

The kind of love that seeks the feelings of a lover

The kind of love that offers security

The kind of love that creates a safe haven

The kind of love that provides peace

The kind of love that subdues storms

The kind of love that rejects fears

The kind of love that responds wisely

The kind of love that honors silence

The kind of love that empowers

The kind of love which dries tears

The kind of love which seeks to soothe

The kind of love which seeks to excite

The kind of love influential enough to change

The kind of love that inspires greatness

The kind of love that produces genuine love

A different kind of love

THE PERFECT HUSBAND

There's one such mode of perfection
A husband
Surprisingly so
He's perfect

He's perfect
To meet her needs
He's perfect
To pray over her

He's perfect
To serve Christ
He's perfect
To kneel before God humbly

He's perfect
To find the woman of God's design
He's perfect
To make her his bride

He's perfect
To sacrifice for his bride
He's perfect
To put God first

He's perfect
To seek God for their needs
He's perfect
To obey God's will

He's perfect
To put her immediately behind Christ
He's perfect
To father their children

He's perfect
To love her with his love whole heart
He's perfect
To invest in her life

He's perfect
To talk to her until she is satisfied
He's perfect
To love her unconditionally

He's perfect
Because He orders his steps
He's perfect
Because he seeks His will

He's perfect
Because He sent her to him
He's perfect
Because he loves her so.

We Are a Love Story

We are a love story
A fairytale
Cinderella even
If you believe in folklore

We were made for each other by Him
Each day He gives me
I will love you
All of you
Each part of you

I love Him
He made you
He made you for me to love
We are truly a love story
Because we believe in Him.

MY KNIGHT AND SHINING ARMOR

In you walked
Wearing your armor
Shiny and new
Critical and confined
A profound spirituality
Your demeanor inspires
Your words challenge
Your intensity attracts
The definition of protection
The example of security
The steward of my needs
The sunshine I respect
In love with life
With authentic laughter
A genuine sense of self
An astounding spirit
An outstanding work ethic
A delicate balance of life work play
A driving energy
A caring appreciation
A dreamy collection of God's best work
The knight you are
The dream you are
     . . . for me.

One Afternoon

One afternoon we fell into a deep love

God sent you me
We befriended one another
We consoled each other
We prayed and prayed
We fasted and fasted
We sought God for His guidance
We invited God's will

God spoke to we
We are accountable to one another
We encourage each other
We study together
We each teach the other
We need each other
We seek each other

God shares you with me
We inspire one another
We compliment
We complement
We read each other's works
We read together
We worship Him together

We fell in love one afternoon
A wonderful, God-designed love
An authentic, God-centered love
A remarkable, God-created love
A profound, God-established love
A residual, God-infused love
A curious, God-filled love

One afternoon, we fell in love
A deep, responsive, God-ordained love

HOLDING MY HAND

When you hold my hand
I think of Him
Could it be that I'm your gift
From Him
(does your presence signify a gift)

When you hold my hand
I'm reconciled to Him
Are you present to minister to the minister
For Him

When you hold my hand
I confess to Him
Are you present to keep me accountable
To Him

When you hold my hand
I supplicate to Him
Could it be that you are my earthly strong tower
Through Him

When you hold my hand
I submit to Him
Are you designed to present me faultless to His throne
In front of Him

When you hold my hand
I thank Him
Could you be my testimony that He remembers me
With Him

When you hold my hand
I feel Him
Are you my bridge
To Him

When you hold my hand
I relax in His arms
Are you my comforter
From Him

When you hold my hand
I see Him
Are you my magnifying glass

To Him

Please keep holding my hand

THE LAYERS OF HIS MUSIC

Just as you listen for certain things in a song
Examine him for those same elements
His layers reflect music quite well
Just peel them back one at a time
He and the layers of his music are the same
The brass blowing
The percussionist keeping time
The strings moving the entire piece forward
Match
      His soul
      His heart
      His mind
Moving mostly in perfect synchronicity
Seeking to reach the unseen
Evoking the most provocative responses
Capturing the hearts—hardened, hurt and broken
Penetrating the innermost aspects of the soul
If you could hear only one instrument at a time
      Which one would capture your heart first?
      Which one keeps you on the edge of your seat?
      Which one addresses your soul?
      Which one soothes your spirit?
So when he talks to you about his goals
      Which melody does he use?
And when he touched your shoulders
      Which harmony did he use?
So when he provoked your smile
      Which baseline did he use?
Inhaled his aroma and stopped your thoughts
      Which chord did you hear?
The thought of his kiss brought a chill over you
      Which song was he playing?

The layers of his music are as varied as
The instruments in any band
Peel them one at a time carefully
      Ever so carefully, examine each layer
Pick the part of the music that creates the
      Most awesome emotional response

Let him reach you
      Like you let the music in
His layers are authentic
      Like the music you let in

His layers profound
       Like the music you enjoy
Enjoy the layers of his music—
       His life, his love, his music

For All Dads:
Tell Her the Truth

Tell her the truth
How to take care of a man
How to kiss that same man
How to love that man
Authentically
Tell her why you love her mother
And will never leave her mother
Tell her why you love her mother
Yet divorced her mother
Tell her why you love her mother
But never married her mother
Correct the misconception
Of her reality
Give her a better view of her reality
She lives there but has no access
Tell her truth
About true love
Tell her how to arrive there
Give her the scoop
Solve the mystery of you
Her decisions are based on what she doesn't know
Tell her the truth
About what she doesn't know
Give her more tools
Enhance her self-esteem
Boost her self-confidence
Give her parts of you
She's never had
Be the dad of her dreams
Be the consultant for her decisions
Be the truth
Give her access to your heart
Give her inroads to your soul
Be her answer
Show her how to relax in the arms of a man
Show her how to argue with a man and
Never lose her cool
Show her how to be her type
Whether type A or not
Remind her that type A is not required
Tell her how to be herself
Help her find what that is
With and without her baby, her mother, her brother

Give her problems to solve
Starting with her own
Give her projects to complete
Starting with herself
Give her the understanding of how you love me
Inside and out
You control that definition and how she defines herself
Help her understand her love language
Help her understand your language
Help her understand your behavior
Be the man in her life
Show her how to keep a man
Show her how to attract a man like you
Or a man you like
Help her understand those sacrifices
You made for her
Tell her the truth
The truth you have never shared
The truth she needs to get out of her rut
Equip her for her future
Redefine her definition of herself
Disconnect and unrelate that definition to her failures of her past
Start answering the why's before she asks
Show her how to survive the p---- war she started
Show her what it takes to have each one of her dreams
Show her how to be a parent
Take her by the hand and show her
Show her a man that is on her side
Help her with her definitions
Of success, love, happiness, joy, peace
Tell her what it means to fall in love
Stop speaking metaphorically
Tell her the why behind your actions
You assume she understands what you do and
What she sees
What about what she doesn't see
What about when she doesn't understand
Show her the end game
Be her best friend
Furnish her a safe place
She's acting out to get your attention
She's calling for you through her behavior
Tell her the truth

THE MEASURE OF A MAN

Man,
        Do you know who you are?
        I asked you a question, Man.
        Answer me!
        You can't answer me?
        That's okay. I'll tell you who you are.

You are my leader, my leadership.
God made you the head and not the tail.

You are my lover.
Christ said love me like He loved the church.
        Sacrificially and sanctified.

You make me perfect.

Christ presented the His church without one spot or wrinkle, made it holy and without blemish and whole.

You teach me love.
God shared 1 Corinthians through you and your actions and deeds and words.

You show me forgiveness.
Christ said we shall forgive seventy times seven, without thought or hesitation.
Thank you for forgiving me.

You are my provider.
God made you to meet my needs and be my comforter and be strong for me because I am the weaker vessel.

God is wise having never made on mistake.
He charged you with my care.
He charged you to love me, like on one else is able or gifted or blessed.

You are her father.
Christ said that children are a gift from God.
When He gives you a child, consider yourself blessed.

Your role is as clear as Waterford crystal, while as heavy and as complex.

God defined you and you can't change His definition.

I know how you can answer me, but more importantly you can answer for yourself who you are.

I love you because of who you are and your submission to His role. Forever.

So who are you?

THE MAN YOU ARE

Strong
Steadfast
Sensitive

Conscientious
Comforting
Caring

Wise
Witty
Warrior

Inquisitive
Insightful
Interesting

Humble
Honest

Lover
Leaders
Loving

Treasure
Tenacious
Timely

Reverent
Rejuvenating
Respected

Nostalgic
Nobel
Natural

Optimistic
Open
Outstanding

Earnest
Energetic

Decisive
Dedicated
Distinguished

The Man You Are

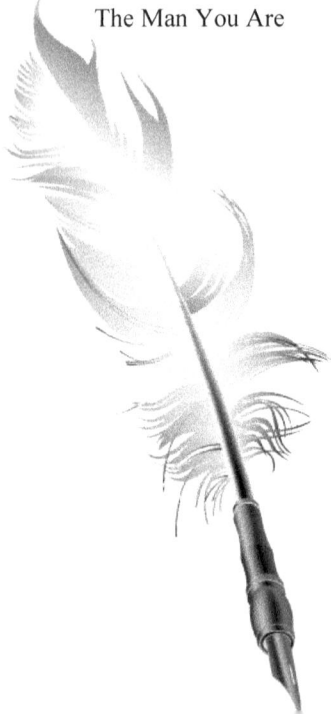

His Glory

The sunlight crept underneath my sheets
Tapped me on my shoulder
Asked me if I still loved you

Perplexed as to why the sun cared
I moved the orchid sheets away from
My morning face to respond

Well Sun, interesting question
Why do you ask

Because each thought is of
Your walks in the park
Your stroll by the lake
Meandering through flowered fields
Swinging to heights higher and higher.

Exchanging glances
Overflowing with affection
Brimming with love
Filled with passion

Sun, still I ask why do you ask?
Well it seems that such a fulfilling
And rewarding love could not
Simply end.

Ending with little resolve.
Makes one wonder what happened

What God has joined
Let no man put asunder

This begs the question
Did God join it?
But when He joined it,
Was if temporary—
Seasonal
Or designed for a lifetime.

Well Sun
Being the magnificent creation
You Are, why don't you ask God?
I'm yet clear.

I don't know why.
Since you asked.

Well my friend
In this life, we ask questions
We receive answers
I stream into your life
To show you God's glory
To offer you God's miracles

God's mercy endures all things
God wants to grant you all
The desires of your heart
If only you would ask
And believe.

Sun, quite frankly I miss him
I do ask why we are apart
I know that I do still love him
But I seek God's direction and
Guidance
On why
And when
But I do love him.

THE MESSAGE

Do the words matter anyway?
Bodies usually gyrating to music
Relative to the rhythm
Never heard those words
The song actually sent a message
Could it be the dialect unclear
Or did the words elude
Definitely misunderstandings develop
Or exist
You missed the message
It was loud
Not particularly clear
Your ears are distracted
Closed to the message
Of love
Of rescue
Of salvation
He sent the car
He sent the bus
He sent the Hummer
He sent the chopper
He sent the jet
You missed the message
Misunderstood the work
Confused about the workers
Unblock the eyes
Unclog the ears
The message is for you
Present yourself to receive
He has gifts through His message

Don't miss anymore of The Message

THINK THINK THINK

Not just for Pooh
You should too
Think, think, think

Before you decide
Before you buy
Before you move
Think, think, think

Thought is important
Almost a skill
Requires practice
Essential still
Think, think, think

Education earned
Accomplishments reached
Goals achieved
Rewards received
Think, think, think

Before you leave
Before you stay
Before you stray
Think, think, think

Ask questions
Ask for advice
Ask for forgiveness
Think, think, think

Think
Think
Think

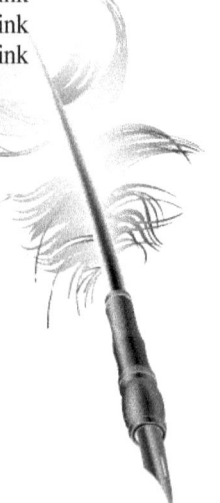

WEARING PINK

I can wear Pink
Even though my breasts are large
      And I am black.

I want you to remember that I sang
      That song
And all the while
You were worrying
About my pink blouse.

YOU HATE AMERICA

But where are you going?

In that country, women wear gear from head to the next person's toe

In that country, children steal, kill and destroy
Can your son pick up an AK-47?
Do you want her to need one?

In that country, the children cannot read
Instead they work as early as they can walk
They understand the definition of poverty
Because they are the definition

In that country, your child would be a prostitute
So that you can eat
You would be the whore but you are too old

In that country, you are the target of military surveillance
You made too many phone calls
Or too much travel
Or too something
The military follows you to the grocery store
And into the bathroom

In that country, storms ravage their homes
Without mercy
Each and every season

In that country, they kill baby girls
But you cannot conceive

In that country, suicide bombers lead the death toll
So much passion for a cause
Even if it is illegal, immoral
Or maybe even stupid
By your standards
But you are all talk

In that country, freedom of speech
Is defined as repeating whatever the government said
Death becomes those who don't
You would've been dead long ago

Are you kidding me?

We are not perfect either
But how can you hate your own soil.

(SO THIS IS) AFRICA

So this is Africa
The substance of your soul
The friction in your spirit
The uncertainty in your voice

A land you don't know well
And you wished it knew you
This vast land possesses your ancestry
Possesses your mind
Possesses you

This land answers all questions
        Of life
        Breath
        Heritage

That Boat
        Held all the life You created
You gave them me
Why?
Who built that damn thing anyway
What cruel soul thought long enough
To create such an ugly space
        . . . the bottom of the bottom of that boat
Where my great-great grandparents
        traveled
        died
Survived from each other's flesh

Pride killed them
Stupidity meant multiplication
Ignorance bred the new strand of this atrocious practice

So when you look at me,
You want to see Africa but can't

If you thought you could send me back,
What would you do?

Africa
        New, different, strong
        And distant

WOULD WE HAVE COME

To this country
Would we have come
Is this US so special
It attracts so many from "foreign lands"

This country has perks
I agree
But would the now us—African Americans—have come
We welcome others but
We are not welcome while native

We were brought at a price
Brought over on a boat
In the bottom of a vessel
Disease transferred
Spiritual destruction begotten
Death resulted

In retrospect
With reflection
After careful reconsideration
Under review
With reservation
Would we have come

Does it really matter
If we turn disenchanted
Where would we go

IN PURPLE INK

The definition of regal
The exhibit of royal
The exercise of intensity
The externalization of an internal passion
The expression of beautiful
The posture of power

When she wrote of love
And only in purple
The question he posed
Started the evolution
Which led a revolution

"Do you write everything in purple?"

"Just the important stuff. The stuff that in designed to last a lifetime. Just the important stuff that influences passion, power, regal and royalty."

Purple
—that one word speaks volumes.

The Glass House In Which We Live

> "If any of you is without sin, let him be the first to throw a stone at her."
>
> John 8:7

Glass houses break
Just throw a stone
Or let a limb fall

Glass houses crack
That crack travels
To create more cracks

Where we live is fragile
And sensitive
Supersensitive
Pliable

Where we live is loving
And warm
Romantic
And sweet

Where we live is powerful
Beyond measure
Resourceful
Creative

Where we live is dynamic
Outstanding
Astounding
Achieving

The glass house in which we live
Is weak
Is shattered
Is irreparable
Is strong
Is resilient

Treat where we live
With care
With honor
And grace
With pride

And respect

The glass house in which we live
Is subtle
And attractive
Is forgiving
And forgiven
Is quiet
And outspoken

Where we live
Requires protection
And nurture
Requests love
And attention
Thrives on affection
And praise

The glass house in which we live
Invites you in to share
The house.

IS LOVE THE BLADE OF GRASS OR THE DRIP OF WATER

When a blade of grass grows through concrete
I wonder if that blade is a model of love.

When a drip of water drips one drop at a time,
This drip eventually causes a crack in this cement,
I wonder if that drip is a model of love.

Is love the blade of grass or the drip of water?

A blade of grass so strong and determined that it breaks through concrete
A love that survives a fight—as strong and determined?

A blade of grass perseveres the trials of reaching the surface
A blade of grass endures the vision of impossibility
Which exists when considering the concrete

A drip that drips so consistently and so patiently—
One drip at a time cracks the concrete
Ever so slowly
Ever so timely

The drip surprises us
The drip overwhelms us
The drip reminds that impossibilities exist
The drip reinvents the possibilities

The blade of grass provides hope for our bleak,
      Tearful moments when love is distant
The blade creates a sense of urgency to revive
      A fallen love
The grass that revives love upon site

The drip causes a split in the concrete
No one repairs that crack
Yet hopes that crack doesn't enlarge
Powerful drip—respected unexpectedly

The blade—impressive, hard to rid
Impossible to forget

If only love followed this model
If only love would persevere the strength of such obstacles

If love could overcome the visibly impossible

When a blade and a drip moves a permanent perception
Love should pay attention, change course and take action
Grass and water have limits
Love knows no bounds

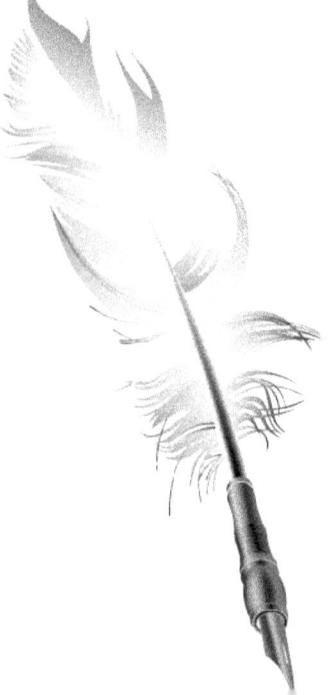

A Warrior Mentality

Love like a warrior
Fight
Eat
All like a warrior

A steel trap—mind your mind
Sharp and strong
Read
Read
Read
Sharpen the mind
Write
Write
Write
Sleep
Eat well
Relax
All like a warrior

Warriors breed warriors
Warriors achieve
A warrior mentality succeeds
A warrior exceeds the minimum standards
Warriors fight
Warriors fight fair
Warriors wage war over injustices

Prepared warrior
Strong warrior
Evident warrior
Caring warrior

Act like a warrior
A warrior attitude
A warrior behavior

A warrior mentality

Perceived Limits

Like calculus—only harder
Which you never really liked anyway
The derivative of frustration
The limit of patience

You can bear more
You can survive more
You can hear more
But do you want to

When you were uncomfortable and confused
In class—it's similar feelings surface
Especially now that you are past calculus
But life presents differently than calculus

Do you consider the effects of "more"
When "more" arrives, do you know if it's "more"
Is it labeled "more" or does it look like the rest of your "stuff"
When "more" arrives do you know how to say no
But can you really say no to "more?"

"More" is the pat on your side from your child
"More" is the care of an ill relative
"More" is the education you need to advance your career

When I didn't think I could go any further—
    I did
When I didn't think I could do anything else—
    I do
When I got tired and thought I would give up—
    I didn't
When I was completely disappointed with my situation—
    I overcame and the disappointment waned

My perceived limits are not just as they seem
But more flexible than my wildest imagination

Do you want to
Bear more
Survive more
Live more
Hear more
Love more
Care more

Do more

Receive new limits
Perceive new limits

THE NERVE TO DREAM

You have the nerve to dream
And expect others to do the same
The audacity

You know dreams don't come true
You know that we don't leave our circumstances
You know that we cannot convince others to believe falsely

You have the nerve and the audacity
To expect us to dream
When there is blight and slums and
Economic hardships

You still dream for better than you have it
Better than <u>all</u> our ancestors
We have more educated
We have more educators
We have more leaders
We have more politicians
We have more wealthy
We have more
. . . yet you still dream of more

You dream that still more can happen
The audacity of you
And the nerve
And the gall of
You to tell our children that they
Can have more than we have
Define more
How much more
More with what?
Less?

Dreams.
You still do it
And in the worst of times
By perception
By the naked eye
But up close they deserve every opportunity to dream
They deserve hopes
They deserve dreams
They deserve the audacity to look at me and
<u>Know</u> that they too can have what we have

And have more of it.

You still dream.

DAYDREAMER

That door leads someplace
Where—yet to be determined
Days I dream the path beyond the door
Each dream diverts differently
Days I dream the door exists to challenge
The solemn space I seek
On the other side
I mix my desires like paint
That door could be purple
Or red or orange or green
Purple declares passion
Red creates power
Orange breeds love
Green lends peace
Days I dream I create the paths
I want
Days I dream my dreams come true
Dreams of passion
Dreams of power
Dreams of love
Dreams of peace
Dreams of days when my dreams meet
Dreams of days when my days feel like dreams
Make my dreams come true so my days and my dreams match
Move me from day dreamer to dream days

IN SEARCH OF

In search of happiness
           Money
           Success
           Fortune
           Fame
           Self

Seeking an identity
        The one within

We seek
We search
We probe
        To find

The one thing that makes us tick
Why I ask
Do we do what we do the way we do?
Often returning void on this journey
To seek for lost treasure
May bring pleasure to some
In search of the self
        We can call our own

In search of

EXAMINE YOUR LIFE

Examine your life
With all its flaws, failures, fatalities
Cross-examine your heart
For answers to the questions your mind ponders

Examine your life
With all its fears, fixations, faults
Cross-examine your mind
For the mysteries your heart encounters

Examine your life
With all its flash, falsehoods, far-reaching
Cross-examine your heart
For all the phobias it sends to the mind

Examine your life
With all the fantasy, funny, foul
Cross-examine your mind
For all the disagreements with your heart

Examine your life
With all its functionality, fabulous, fancy
Cross-examine your heart
For all the mixed messages sent to your mind

Examine your life
With all its feisty, frightening, fiery
Cross-examine your mind
For all the commonalities shared with your heart

After all that . . . LIVE A WHOLE LIFE.

SHEDDING THE STUFF

Put down the stuff
Discard the stuff
Give it up
Turn it loose

How long did it take to collect that stuff
How long have you had that stuff
How are you keeping up with that stuff
How much does that stuff weigh
How does that stuff help you or others

Doesn't it hurt to carry that around
Does that prevent you from moving swiftly
Does it prevent you from making good choices
Doesn't it distract you from your purpose

What is that stuff you carry around
What do you do with that stuff
What prevents you from putting it down
What keeps you committed to the stuff
What makes that stuff so important

When do you have the time to manage this stuff
When do you have the energy to manage this stuff
When do you collect that stuff
When did you realize that you had this much stuff

Where have you traveled with this stuff
Where do you keep this stuff
Where have you collected this stuff from

Do you think that your burdens are better because you still have them
Has anyone ever asked you for any of this stuff
Have you considered the benefit or burden of maintaining all of this stuff
Have you considered the burdens of this stuff

How long before you give it up
When do you suspect that you can release that stuff
What will it take to release this stuff
Where do you want to deposit this stuff
Who can help you loose yourself of this stuff

Put it down
Discard the stuff

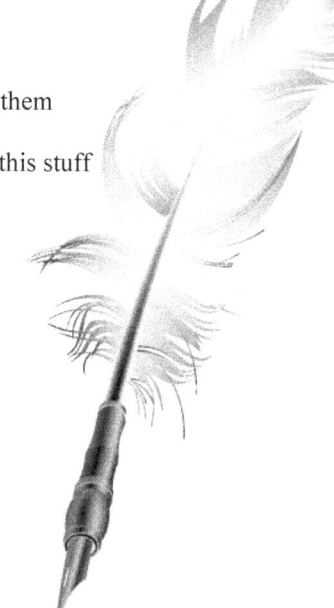

Give it up

Shed the stuff

LIFE HAPPENS

life happens
oh yes it does
just one excuse
you could be loose from the
destiny you should have

walk in between the drops
the drops of disappointment
drops of despair
of decisions gone south

live between the drops
live happily
live fully
live graciously
live wealthy

life happens
oh yes it does
stand strong—have courage
be decisive—have faith
focus, focus, focus on the positive

change develops during the drops
change blooms between the drops
change your situation before your situation changes you

between the drops
great decisions are made
discoveries lie ahead
love generated

the drops never stop
but the umbrella you use
to cover your head will
make your journey easier

between the drops
find shelter for the rainy days

Mirror, Mirror

"Mirror, mirror
On the wall
Who's the fairest of them all?"

Who talks to a mirror
Expecting some other version of the truth
Mirror, am I pretty today?
Better question
Yet confused about the source

Mirror, is my hurt obvious?
Or, Mirror, do you see my love?
Mirror, is my heart showing?
Or, Mirror, is my brain in view?

"Mirror, mirror
On the wall
Who's the fairest of them all?"

Who talks to a mirror
Expecting some other version of the lies
We hear from others
Mirror, why doesn't he like me?
Mirror, why doesn't he love me?
Better question
Yet benefit irrelevant

"Mirror, mirror
On the wall
Who's the fairest of them all?"

Who talks to a mirror
Expecting some other version of the truth
Versus the lies we tell ourselves
Mirror, treat me special, please
Mirror, tell me all is well
Mirror, tell me how to have a better life
Mirror, what answers do you have for me today?
Better questions exist

Who talks to a mirror anyway
Expecting the reality to change
Because you asked a mirror.

THE MIRACLE BEFORE YOU

Miracles happen daily
        Somewhere
Miracles are real
        Everyday
Do you see them
Do you experience them
Do you believe in them
Do you need a miracle
Are you a miracle

The miracle before you
Is real
The miracle before you
        Breathes
        Speaks
        Listens
        Cries
        Screams
        Fears
        Fails
        Falters
        Succeeds

Do you show up
        To receive the miracle
Miracles happen

Do you show up
        To be the miracle
Miracles require presence

Do you show up
        To witness the miracle
Miracles require action

Miracles are presents
The undeserved reward of change
The unwarranted gift of mercy

Don't miss the miracle

THE SALT FROM YOUR TEARS IS HYPERTENSIVE

Have you tasted the salt of your tears?
Real salty
So salty that pressure results
Scientifically impossible
Physically possible

Consider the tears
Joyful
Sadness
Happiness
Hurt
Hope
Fears

Tears cleanse
Tears rejuvenate
Tears gives closure
Tears clear
Tears create

Real salty though

How do we reconcile the two

Cleansing coupled with reconciliation
Through the salty tears
Salt
An addictive flavor
      To the taste
Not for the spirit

Don't taste all of the tears.

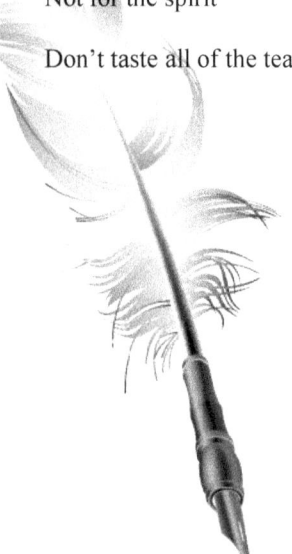

NINETY OR SOMETHING CLOSE

Life is too short to be this weak
To go it alone
Weaknesses exist
Yes, life is short
Ninety years is not a long time
For support of my goals
Or yours
Yet it seems eternal
When each day is unbearable

When this life is complete
All we have is the memories we share
The love we make
Or is it the reverse
The memories we make
The love we share

Being weak in this world
Alone in this world
Shouldn't qualify under a great life
Coupled with someone who may love
With such specific conditions
That impossibility sets in
The impossibility of strength
The impossibility of forgiveness
The impossibility of a shared quality of life

Life is too short
To live life
With built in mediocrity
To be this weak
And go it alone.

Ninety is a long time to
Bear ridiculous conditional love.

BORROWED TIME

Not in my hands
Life or death
Days are numbered
The hour unknown

Each day is more than I deserve
Not even the rest of this day is promised
But worse than a loan
Time cannot be repayed

Time is a gift
A gift to be cherished
Cherishing life is paramount
The life He designed

The next breath I take
Is not my own
Not promised
Yet purposed

I am on borrowed time
Time I cannot repay
No amortization schedule available
Just do the work assigned

Do all the work assigned
No complaints
No worries
Not necessarily fair

Borrowed time
On loan for a season
Life is lived according to His will
Live life with a cause

Act like it's borrowed
It's not yours to do with as you please
Remember it's borrowed
It <u>all</u> belongs to Him!

We live on borrowed time.

Clear the Mechanism

Quiet so I CAN focus
Stop speaking negative thoughts into my being

QUIET so I can focus
Stop delivering the negative you hope I adopt

Quiet so I can FOCUS
Stop filling me with stuff that falters my progress

Quiet so I can focus
Stop calling me out of my name

CLEAR the mechanism
Clear THE mechanism
Clear the MECHANISM

Clear my mind for the "stuff" that
        Needs my focus

Clear my heart for the "stuff" that
        Requires my attention

Clear my soul for the "stuff" that
        Qualifies for commitment

CLEAR the mechanism
Clear THE mechanism
Clear the MECHANISM

When the world is rambunctious around me
Clear the mechanism

When the world rejects me
Clear the mechanism

When the world reacts negatively to the good I do
Clear the mechanism

While the world is questioning who I am
Clear the mechanism

While the world is asking why I am
Clear the mechanism

When the world is asking why I do what I do
Clear the mechanism

When the world is asking how I do what I do
Clear the mechanism

Clear the mechanism

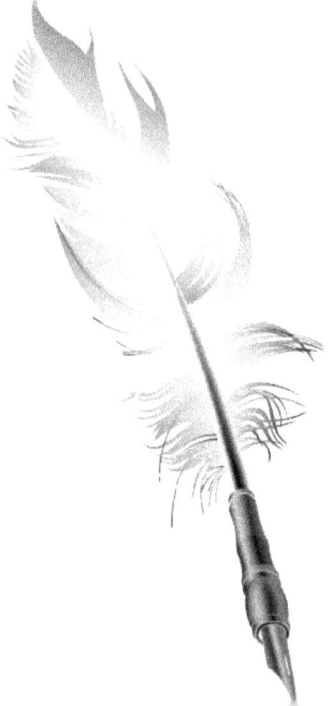

LEGEND OF BAGGER VANCE—

Focus
Focus   Focusing
Focus   Focused
Authentic Swing
Find yours
Equipped
I lost my swing
Life's answers to your burden
        Require your attention
             Your focus
             Your focus
             Your focus
This started off about golf
But is it really that far—
        Life I mean

The authenticity of a perfect swing
Which searches for each of us.

DECLARATION OF INDEPENDENCE

Is it worth all that
Such huge sacrifice
Such little satisfaction

A little injection
A small glass
One pill

All life altering life's alternative

Crawl
Walk
Run
        Away from that substance
        That abusive substance
        The body—altering
        The mind—changing substances

Liquid that calls your name
        Name in the midst of your storm
Promising to save you from your troubles
Never to deliver

Turn away from your name
Deny self
Reject instant gratification

Raise the bar
Your standards define your character

Your declaration of independence is today.

Forgiven

When are you forgiven,
        Forgiving should be natural
How long do you hold a grudge?
        That grudge is infectious
How long have you been living in your own
        Unforgiveness?
When was the last time you forgave yourself?
When do you anticipate forgiving yourself again?

The ability to forgive
And desire shouldn't be mixed
Can you forgive?
Can you forget?
Will the relationship recover?

The inability to forgive
Coupled with the desire to love
Equals a deathly combination
How deathly?

Loving with forgiveness
Quite rewarding
Sometimes overwhelming
        Awesome reflection
        Definition of commitment

Forgiveness is circular
        Forgiving
                Forgiven

IN TWENTY MINUTES

Who will remember
  Those words
  That stuff
  That drama
    In twenty minutes

Who will know
  That information
  Those details
  The events
    In twenty minutes

Who will care
  About that outfit
  About that dwelling
  About the transportation
    In twenty minutes

Within twenty minutes
  Life avails it treasures
  Life shares its tragedies
  Life gifts us with wisdom
  Life equips us with knowledge

In twenty minutes
  Who will care

ATTITUDE IN STANZAS

Are you serious
Yes, you have an attitude
Positive vs. negative—not the point
Your attitude was within these stanzas

Your attitude is evident in the stanza
Your sadness peeked through in the first stanza
Your tears were evident in the second line
Your fear jumped out of the second stanza

In one stanza you expressed your love
In another, you expressed your discontent
Certainly you shared your anger in a few
Your love is most evident in the stanzas

What bravery to share on paper your heart
What transparency to declare your loss in print
How classy of you to disclose your hurts
How courageous of you to reveal your pains

But after all that you remain loveable
And in spite of that pain you reach out to others
Because of your pain you have become more compassionate to others
In that your attitude has improved

Your stanzas evolved into our lifestyles
Your words infected our hearts
Your compassion reaches others
Your love moves mountains

You shared your attitude in stanzas
Something most of us will never do

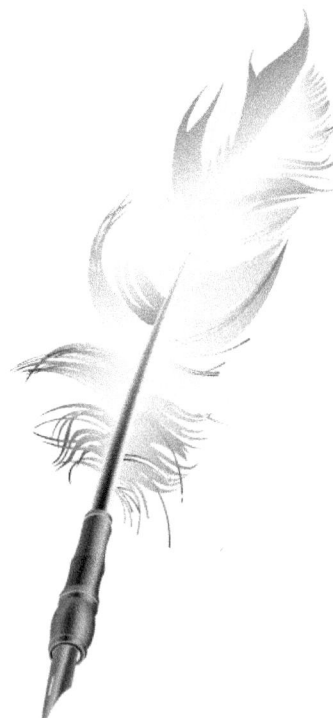

LADY IN WAITING

Ladies wait
Real ladies patiently wait
Not that the proposed waiting
Wait on love
Wait on answers
On proposals
On dreams to come true
Cinderella-ish indeed
Never reality based
Waiting on approval
Waiting on difference
Ladies wait
Ladies wait on excellence
Ladies wait on solutions
Ladies wait with expectancy
Ladies wait on the truth
Ladies wait on the end result
Ladies wait

PUZZLES

Pieces that should fit together just so
Made to match
Designed to move your mind
Puzzles not designed to confuse

Put them together two pieces at a time
Build them to create a picture
Of love
Or chocolates
Or whatever else you've seen on a puzzle
Including you
That photo is one process away from
A puzzle
In a need of solving

Put the pieces together
To complete the whole
Placed together with love
Care
Concern
Trust
Interlock the pieces to
Reveal the best of the puzzle.

HEART CHECK

It may be that you need a heart check
Could it be that your heart is missing
The essentials that hearts require
Have you had that checked
The heart is a major organ
The brain is important
It's supposed to control the heart
I beg to differ, really
When the heart malfunctions
The brain does some weird stuff too
The brain then affects the rest of the body
The heart chooses the attitude
The heart changes the mind
The heart charges the ambition
The heart cheers the spirit
The heart challenges the decisions
Check the heart regularly
The heart needs maintenance
The heart deserves a check
The heart may hurt
But can heal
The heart may be sad
But can laugh
Check the heart
It's where the love develops

IN MY SHOES

Walk around in my shoes
The way you try shoes on
Walk around awhile in my shoes
Are they too tight
Are they too loose
Too short
Too long
Too busy
Too plain

In my shoes
There is excellence
There are achievements
There is motivation
There are disappointments
There are tears
There are standards

In my shoes
There is struggle
There is triumph
There is perfection
There is creativity
There is progress

In my shoes
There is love
There is compassion
There is power
There is wisdom
There is determination
There is drive
There is discipline

Don't envy my shoes
You don't know how they fit
You don't know how they feel
You don't know where these feet have been

Don't envy my shoes
You will have to take the successes
Along with the failures
You will have to take the pain
Along with the joy

You will have to take the happiness
Along with the disappointment

In my shoes requires
Focus
Attention to detail
Attitude of excellence

Be careful what you envy
Be careful what you ask for
Be careful what you consider great

In my shoes.

Visit Life's Edge

Each one different
The edge that is
Your limits may
Resemble mine
Yet differently composed

Escape life's boundaries
Visit the edge
The edge of love
The edge of joy
The edge of peace

Escape life's mediocrity
Attack the edge
The edge of bliss
The edge of wonder
The edge of wow

Distant from life's failures
Encounter the edge
The edge of achievement
The edge of excitement
The edge of acceptance

The edge is dangerous
The life's edge demands discomfort
The life's edge requires abandonment
The life's edge reprimands fear

The life's edge achieves
The life's edge accomplishes
The life's edge deepens

Visit the life's edge
Stay there for fuel
The life's edge stimulates
The life's edge grow
The life's edge elevates

The life's edge
—go there
—go there often.

THE SCENT OF YOUR FEET

I want to smell your feet
In the comfortable
Unspoken communication
Of silence

The comfort ability of love
Immersed in the connection
That golden moment

The love we share
Absent conversation
Minus pretense
Defines authentic
Defies falsehoods
I took your shoes off
To smell your feet
I want to smell your feet
I want to smell your
External foundation
Your transportation
Intrigues me
Feet don't have a great reputation

The Heartbeat and Its Version of the Story

And when you thought your senses
Gave you up for the last time
Your heart beat goes on to tell the rest

The rapid heart beat tells the story
That your mouth stifles and stops
Right at the edge of your teeth
Right at the tip of your tongue

But the heart beat cannot be disguised
The heart beat cannot be extinguished
The heart beat speeds and slows based
On feelings
Driven by thought
Stimulated by actions
Reconciled by dreams

All captured by love

The heartbeat tells the story
The story the mouth censures
The story that the mind hopes to dismiss
The dialogue that eyes tries to avoid
The story that the body ignores

The heart beat tells the story
The whole story
The truth
And nothing but the truth.

SEPARATING MEMORIES FROM REALITY

In those old photos
Were you really happy
Was that simply a photo opportunity
At that party
Did you think that life would be better
Eventually
Eventually never came

In those old photos
Did you redefine happy
Did you sacrifice happy for
A fake peace
Or a secure habitat
Do you even know how to experience
I mean really know when happy
Has existed awhile
What do you really do

Well take those old photos
Take another look
Focus on the eyes
Those eyes checked the room
For comfort
For strength
For security
They landed alone

In those old photos
Reality set in
You accepted those mediocre memories
That we dressed up as all that you deserve

Wish reality more
Closely resembled genuine memories
Where happiness is the standard and not the goal
The next to impossible
Nearly never achieved
Clearly desired
Distorted definition of happiness.

Until then pop the photo smile on
Until it's the reality you deserve.

Transfer On Death

Give it to me
No it's mine
Momma told me that was mine
She left you that stuff over there
Transfer on death

Too much struggle
Too much pain
Life reduced to stuff,
Sentiments
Worldly possessions
Junk
Causes huge arguments
Fights
Scuffles
Silence
That could last for years

Why pursue stuff
Did you pursue the relationship
With the same fervor as that set of dishes
You didn't even visit her
But here you are to retrieve her stuff
Transfer on death is not optional
How we handle it is quite optional

Why do we want that "stuff" anyway
Is it valuable
Is it old
Is it yours

Why do you feel entitled to something
That was never yours
With which you have no relationship
To which you have no loyalty

It's just stuff
Simple
Replaceable
Fragile
Stuff

All is transferable upon death.

THE FAMILY SECRETS

Lies
Deceit
Bastards
Disease
Illness
Death
Abortion
Miscarriage
Traditions
      —stolen, borrowed, unique
Infidelity

So many secrets
So many lies
Too many secrets
Can not get past lies

Who knows the people
Who you called parents
When they don't reveal the truth
A different life revealed—
Lead to different results—
      Maybe, maybe not.

The family secrets
Who keeps them
And why?

Who reveals them?
And when?

Why keep them?
Who needs them?

The life that could be mine
Hindered by the family secrets.

THE ONE QUESTION I HAVE

God if only one question I had, it would be . . .
Why did You save my life?
What do You want me to do?
What do You think of me?
Why do You love me so?
What do You consider my greatest attribute?
What do You need me to do?
Who do You want to me to serve?
What do I need to do to please You?
Why do You forgive me still?
Why did You call me to serve You?
Who do You want me to seek out?
Who would You like me to meet?
How can I make You happy?

I just have one question
I just want to know
How I can stop grieving you?
I love You.

The One Question I have:
How can I love You more?

In Purple Ink

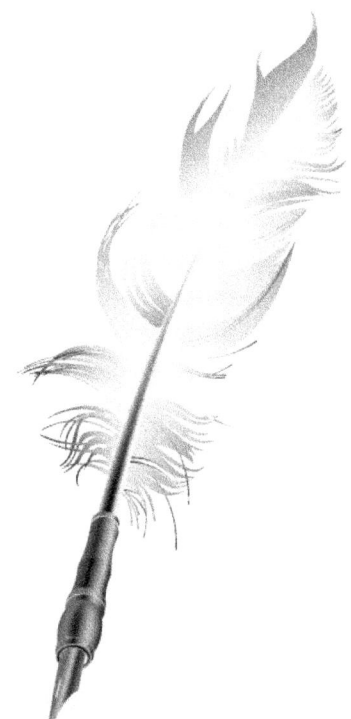

In Purple Ink

ACKNOWLEDGEMENTS

God, thank You for Your plans for me. Thank You for ***In Purple Ink: Poetry for the Spirit*** and choosing me to complete Your project. I just want to please You. Thank You for continuing to anoint me and to invest in me and my gifts, which keep surprising me. Thank You for loving and forgiving me.

Hillary and Nehemiah, thank you for enduring my late nights, your ideas, the sounding board, the love and the support. Thank you for loving me, especially when I do nothing without a pen and a clipboard.

To my editor, Ronald Williams. Thanks for the feedback and the discussions. The honesty was quite powerful and has grown me and my writing. Thanks for enforcing the standard. Thank you for understanding my words, thoughts and images.

To my photographer, Ray Carrington, III. Thanks for the great images of me. I am grateful for your influence in my life. Thank you for showing up at my events and attaching great memories to them all.

To my graphic artist, Ron Nicholson and Picture Perfect Designs. Thanks for the art and imagination, for making my words look fabulous. Thank you for your patience and vivid imagination.

To my prayer partners and to my accountability partners, thank you for the long talks and the powerful prayers and the encouragement.

To the persons who this will reach and empower and touch and affect, may these words empower you and help you reach some resolve. May you be inspired to achieve your goals and dreams. May you enhance your relationships with God so that your other relationships will also improve. May you enhance your self-esteem through prayer and studying. May you have courage and peace. Share love the best you can until you can share love without reservation.

ABOUT THE AUTHOR

Minister Onedia N. Gage has been writing since age 13. She has written through each of her storms and her sunshine. The gift of writing is ever present in her life. She is often seen with a pad and pen. Rev. Gage is truly transparent in her writings and seeks to share her testimony with others. She offers her testimony through the pages she authors.

As We Grow Together Daily Devotional for Expectant Couples addresses Christian parenting. There is an accompanying **As We Grow Together Prayer Journal for Expectant Couples**.

The Blue Print, poetry that exposes her innermost thoughts, was developed over 15 years. She encourages the creativity in others and is starting a writing circle for those who write. She desires to turn what has previously been a hobby into full-time career.

In Purple Ink: Poetry for the Spirit captures the essence of the journey through pain and reconciliation to God. The road away from pain is a complicated one so she offers this work to insure that you are not alone and certainly not forgotten.

The Measure of a Woman: The Details of Her Soul discloses the secrets and the nuances and the idiosyncrasies of a woman. **Measure** is bold and states clearly that we are more than conquerors and the journey of a woman will certainly show her worth.

On This Journey Daily Devotional for Young People covers issues young people struggle with daily. Because there is a shortage of resources which exist for the sole purpose of assisting our young people with biblical sources for worldly situations, Rev. Gage designed **OTJ** for that purpose. **On This Journey Prayer Journal for Young People** offers young people the opportunity to journal their prayers and concerns in a format comfortable for them.

She authored **Promises, Promises**, a novel, out a need for female heroines of her time.

Her life philosophy is three – fold: A) "What have you done today to invest in your future?" B) Reading is essential to your positive contribution to our community; and, C) "If not me, who? If not now, when?" She feels her time is best spent when youth benefit from her experiences.

Minister Gage was licensed as a minister June, 2009. She is an active member of The Church Without Walls where she is on the clergy team, the women's ministry, facilitates various small group Bible studies, has served with children's ministry and Vacation Bible School.

Her community efforts are commendable as a Board of Directors of YMCA-Northeast, Houston, Living Forward Alliance and Spaulding for Children. Because of her volunteerism with the Houston Area Urban League's NULITES, she was elected one of the youngest board members of the Houston Area Urban League. She is also a member of Zeta Phi Beta Sorority, Inc., National Council of Negro Women, Toastmasters, International, Top Ladies of Distinction, and "Sistah to Sistah," a literary review group.

Onedia N. Gage is a native Houstonian. She is a graduate of Kaplan University with a Masters in Business Administration, Lamar University with a Masters in Education in Education Administration, and University of Houston, central campus, with a Bachelor's of Science degree in Economics and a minor in African American Studies. She is a graduate of Bellaire Senior High School. She is currently pursuing her Ph. D. in Business Leadership and Masters of Arts in Christian Education.

She is has two beautiful children.

Please feel free to contact her at www.onediagage.com and Onediagage@onediagage.com.

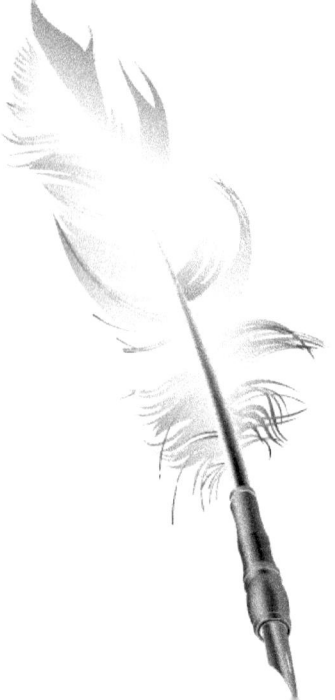

ISBN: 978-0-9801002-5-9

www.ingramcontent.com/pod-product-compliance
Lightning Source LLC
Chambersburg PA
CBHW032055150426
43194CB00006B/538